Tracey Fern · Pictures by Boris Kulikov

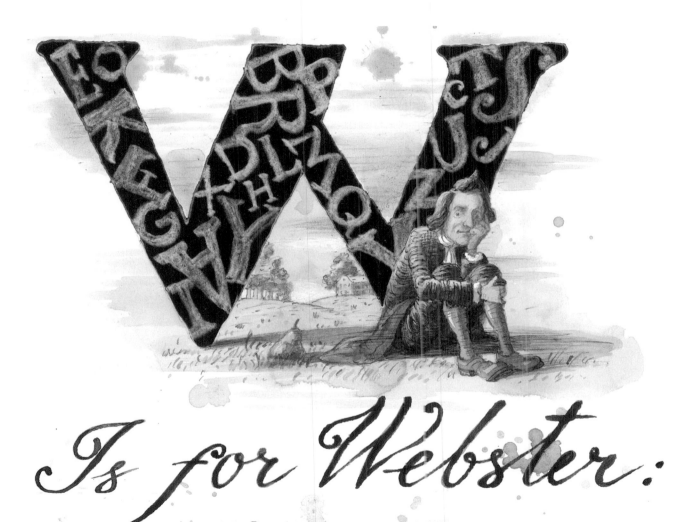

Is for Webster:

Noah Webster
and His American Dictionary

Margaret Ferguson Books

FARRAR STRAUS GIROUX · NEW YORK

Right from an early age, Noah Webster was an odd fellow. He was tall and skinny. He had brilliant red hair. He liked to talk big. And he loved learning. But Noah did not love his one-room school in West Hartford, Connecticut.

Noah's school was in session only a few months a year, between autumn harvest and spring planting. It had hardly any books. There was no homework. And most of the school day was spent goofing around. Noah called goofing around "playing roguish tricks." This is an example of Noah talking big.

Noah begged his pa to send him to a school with lots of work and books and hardly any goofing around. His pa knew Noah would make a terrible farmer. Noah spooked the cows by reciting Latin and spent too much time reading *Ames' Almanack* under the apple trees.

So in 1774, when Noah was sixteen, his pa took out
a loan on the farm, lent Noah a swayback mare, and
sent him off to Yale College in nearby New Haven.

Yale was in session all year round, had lots
of books, expected students to rise at 5:30 a.m.
and study two hours before breakfast, and fined
students two shillings for making "tumult,
noise, hallooing," or otherwise goofing around.
Noah thought Yale was wonderful.

Several months after Noah arrived at Yale, the chapel bells began to toll. The Revolutionary War had begun! The American colonies began fighting for their independence from Britain.

Noah volunteered to fight the British in New York. Although he was never in a battle, Noah was "ill able to bear the fatigues of a soldier." That was Noah's big way of saying he was a lousy soldier. So even though the war was still going on, Noah returned to Yale.

Noah graduated in 1778 with no money and no job. What would he do for work? How would he survive? Noah went home to think.

"I can do no more for you," Pa told Noah sadly. He gave Noah a handful of shillings and asked him to leave home to find work. Noah set off alone, "overwhelmed with gloomy apprehensions." That was Noah's big way of saying he was afraid.

So Noah did the only thing he knew how to do: he went back to school, this time as a schoolmaster. Noah taught in schools in Connecticut and New York. Everywhere, Noah thought the schools were "wretched" and the British textbooks being used were "defective and erroneous." That was Noah's way of saying they stunk.

Noah believed schools should have American books that would appeal to American children. His students were from many different countries and cultures—they were Dutch, French, German, Scottish, Danish, Swedish, Irish, and more. They didn't look alike, think alike, or act alike. They didn't even speak English alike!

By now, the Revolutionary War was winding down. It was clear that America would win its independence. Noah was a proud patriot who longed to do something that would help to hold his new, complicated nation together. Being a bit of a know-it-all, Noah thought he knew just what America needed: its own language—one different from the English spoken in Britain.

"A national language is a national tie," Noah insisted to all who would listen, and to many who wouldn't.

Noah knew he was just the man to give America its own language. He would start with a
speller. Of course, Noah gave it a fancy name: *A Grammatical Institute of the English Language*. His
speller was tiny, only six inches tall and three inches wide. But for a little book, it had some big
ideas—ideas that were totally different from those in British spellers.

Noah included everyday words like *scab*, *grub*, and *mop*. He simplified the spelling of many
words, sometimes deleting extra letters that weren't pronounced or spelling words the way they
sounded. He put pictures on every page. He grouped words that rhymed. He filled the pages
with stories about American patriots. He bound the book in bright blue. And he sold it for
only fourteen shillings.

Noah rode on horseback, stopping at each village crossroad and cobblestoned square. Everywhere, he peddled his "blue-backed speller." Noah sold out the first five thousand copies in nine months. Printers kept printing it. People kept buying it. Noah's speller was a bestseller.

He still wasn't satisfied. His speller was surely a good start, but it was too small and simple. Noah wanted to give America its own dictionary, a patriotic dictionary that also included America's own unique words.

Noah needed to support himself while he wrote his dictionary. He loved to hear himself talk about his ideas and figured other people would love to hear him talk, too. So Noah put on his best (and only) waistcoat and buckled slippers and set out again, traveling up and down the coast from Connecticut to South Carolina to New Hampshire and back. Along the way, Noah sold his speller and lectured about his dictionary idea to anyone who would pay two shillings to hear him speak.

Many folks found Noah annoying. They called him the "Monarch" because of his know-it-all ways. It was a harsh nickname in a country that had just fought a war to toss a monarch out.

They picked on everything about Noah, from his prickly personality to his "porcupine" hair. One reviewer even complained that the portrait of Noah in his speller was so ugly it would frighten children away from learning to read.

Most people not only didn't like Noah, they didn't like his dictionary idea either.

Many people thought the English language would be ruined if he took out British words that weren't used in America and replaced them with words used only in America. Noah thought words were like the leaves of a tree: old ones drop off and new ones grow.

"New words! New ideas!" Noah mocked. "Why, the man is mad!"

Noah was joking, but most folks weren't laughing. They stopped calling him the Monarch and started calling him the Lunatic.

One of the few people who didn't think Noah was crazy was Rebecca Greenleaf—"the lovely Becca," Noah called her. So Noah married Becca. They settled down in Connecticut and eventually had eight children.

In 1806, Noah published a small dictionary for students and travelers. Once again, Noah chose a big name: *A Compendious Dictionary of the English Language*. It was a flop, but Noah wasn't discouraged.

He started working on his big dictionary in 1807. He had already researched some words for his speller and his small dictionary. His big dictionary needed to be even better. He searched many famous British dictionaries, from *A Table Alphabeticall of Hard Usual English Wordes* to Dr. Samuel Johnson's *A Dictionary of the English Language*, writing down all the useful words he found—except those that he thought were just too rude. Then he added words that were used only in America.

Next, Noah traced the roots of each word. Many English words originally came from other languages, and Noah wanted his dictionary to include every word's origin. Finally, Noah wrote just the right definition, often using quotations from famous Americans like Ben Franklin and George Washington to show the different meanings of words.

Noah guessed his big dictionary would take him five years to finish—eight to ten years at the very most.

Five years later, Noah was still on the letter *A*.

He didn't want to give up on his dictionary, but he had to find a way to feed the lovely Becca and their children. He tried teaching, writing essays, practicing law, and editing a newspaper. At each job and in every town, Noah managed to annoy someone with his ideas. And nowhere was he able to spend enough time working on his dictionary.

"What can I do?" Noah wrote to his friend Josiah Quincy, in a mood as black as his silk stockings. "I shall sell my house to get bread for my children." He signed his name, "Yours in low spirits."

In 1812, low-spirited Noah sold his expensive house and bought a humble farmer's cottage in Amherst, Massachusetts. He raised white-spotted cows named Gentle and Comfort, because he needed some gentle comfort, and grew apples, pears, peaches, and prized potatoes to feed his family.

It was time to work on his dictionary again.

Noah set up a study in a large corner room on the second floor of the cottage. He packed the walls with sand to keep out the shouts and stomps of his children. Any who dared to enter the study, however, were immediately treated to raisins and peppermints.

Noah filled his study with hundreds of books that he had collected over the years. He built a circular desk, two feet wide, and loaded it with dictionaries in twenty languages. He surrounded himself with words.

Every morning, Noah rose just after dawn.
"Up, up, children!" he called.

Noah said his prayers and had breakfast
with his lovely Becca and children. Then he
spent his days standing in the center of his desk,
turning around and around inside the circle,
tracing the origins and meanings of words.

It was enough to make most men dizzy. But
it stirred Noah's heart—from sixty to eighty-
five beats a minute, to be exact. Noah—the odd
fellow—knew this because he took his pulse after
every exciting discovery!

By 1822, Noah had done all the research he could from the books in his study.

He traveled to several American libraries to use their books and then moved his family to New Haven so that he could use the Yale library.

He had reached the letter *R*, but he had had to skip the origin of many words. There were simply no books in America that were old enough to help him understand where many words came from.

In 1824, Noah sold most of his library, borrowed money from one of his now-grown-up daughters, bundled up hundreds of handwritten pages, and sailed for Europe.

At the National Library in Paris and at the University of Cambridge in England, Noah finally found the books he needed. His heart pounded triple-time in delight!

In 1825, almost twenty years after he first started writing, Noah carefully wiped his quill and snugged the cork in his ink bottle. His dictionary—more than 70,000 entries—was complete.

Noah's *An American Dictionary of the English Language* was the largest English dictionary ever written. Many people also thought it was the best English dictionary ever written.

By now, America had changed. Andrew Jackson was president, and he was both a common man and a bad speller. The nation was finally ready for Noah's dictionary, full of common words simply spelled.

States issued congratulatory proclamations. Newspapers called him "America's own Dr. Webster." Congress adopted Noah's dictionary as its standard reference book. And although Noah's dictionary has been revised many times, it is still the standard in America today.

Noah created a new American language for a new American nation. And Noah became an American hero. You can see for yourself—under *W* for *Webster*.

Webster, Noah *(1758–1843) United States lexicographer and writer.*

Author's Note

Photo courtesy of Yale University Manuscripts & Archives.

Noah Webster was born on October 16, 1758. Right from the start, Noah wasn't just odd, he was smart. He loved to learn and spoke and wrote about many subjects, including politics, education, economics, religion, science, and vegetable manure! He studied several languages. He was a lawyer, newspaper editor, and justice of the peace. He served in the Connecticut and Massachusetts legislatures. He helped found Amherst College. But mostly, Noah loved words.

Noah's dictionary is still the most popular dictionary in the United States. It has been updated many times since 1828, with Noah and later editors often adding and deleting words, and then sometimes adding them back in, as words fell into and out of use. People still say, "Look in *Webster's*," when they mean, "Look in the dictionary." Noah would have defined *Webster's* to mean "dictionary" or, more likely, "extraordinary, stupendous, and unique dictionary!"

Noah especially loved his own words, and he wrote many of them in long letters. Some of these letters, and the source of several quotes in this book, are contained in *Letters of Noah Webster*, edited with an introduction by Harry R. Warfel (New York: Library Publishers, 1953). The definition of *Noah Webster* was taken from *Webster's New Explorer Desk Encyclopedia* (Springfield, Mass.: Federal Street Press, 2003). Titles of some of the works referred to in this book have been shortened or simplified, since in the spirit of Noah, the complete titles are often exceedingly big.

Additional sources are as follows:

Kendall, Joshua. *The Forgotten Founding Father: Noah Webster's Obsession and the Creation of an American Culture*. New York: G. P. Putnam's Sons, 2010.

Lepore, Jill. "Noah's Mark." *The New Yorker* (6 November 2006): 78.

Micklethwait, David. *Noah Webster and the American Dictionary*. Jefferson, N.C.: McFarland & Company, Inc., Publishers, 2000.

Noah Webster House and West Hartford Historical Society. www.noahwebsterhouse.org.

Unger, Harlow Giles. *Noah Webster: The Life and Times of an American Patriot*. New York: John Wiley & Sons, Inc., 1998.

Warfel, Harry R. *Noah Webster: Schoolmaster to America*. New York: The Macmillan Company, 1936.

To my late father, Daniel Fern, who loved words, too —T.F.

For Sherchuk and Peter and Larisa Konnikov —B.K.

Farrar Straus Giroux Books for Young Readers
175 Fifth Avenue, New York 10010

Text copyright © 2015 by Tracey Fern
Pictures copyright © 2015 by Boris Kulikov
All rights reserved
Color separations by Bright Arts (H.K.) Ltd.
Printed in China by RR Donnelley Asia Printing Solutions Ltd.,
Dongguan City, Guangdong Province
Designed by Kristie Radwilowicz
First edition, 2015
1 3 5 7 9 10 8 6 4 2

mackids.com

Library of Congress Cataloging-in-Publication Data
Fern, Tracey E., author.
    W is for Webster : Noah Webster and his American dictionary / Tracey Fern ; pictures by
Boris Kulikov.
        pages cm
    Summary: "A picture book biography of Noah Webster"—Provided by publisher.
    ISBN 978-0-374-38240-7
    1. Webster, Noah, 1758–1843—Juvenile literature.   2. Lexicographers—United States—
Biography—Juvenile literature.   3. English language—United States—Lexicography—
Juvenile literature.   4. Educators—United States—Biography—Juvenile literature.
I. Kulikov, Boris, 1966–illustrator.   II. Title.

PE64.W5F46 2015
423.092—dc23
[B]
                                                                                            2015002962

Farrar Straus Giroux Books for Young Readers may be purchased for business or promotional
use. For information on bulk purchases please contact Macmillan Corporate and Premium Sales
Department at (800) 221-7945 x5442 or by email at specialmarkets@macmillan.com.